THE GREAT SECRET

Health, Beauty, Happiness, Friend - Making, Common Sense, Success

By
Francis Edward Clark, D.D.
President of the United Society of Christian Endeavor and of the World's Christian Endeavor Union

"The secret of the Lord is with them that fear him."

First Fruits Press
Wilmore, Kentucky
c2015

The great secret : health, beauty, happiness, friend - making, common sense, success, by Francis Edward Clark.

First Fruits Press, ©2015
Previously published: Boston, Chicago : United Society of Christian Endeavor ©1897.

ISBN: 9781621713470 (print), 9781621713487 (digital)

Digital version at http://place.asburyseminary.edu/christianendeavorbooks/8/

Clark, Francis E. (Francis Edward), 1851-1927.
    The great secret : health, beauty, happiness, friend - making, common sense, success / by Francis Edward Clark.
    102 pages ; 21 cm.
    Wilmore, Ky. : First Fruits Press, ©2015.
    Reprint. Previously published: Boston : United Society of Christian Endeavor ©1897.
    ISBN: 9781621713470 (pbk.)
    1. Conduct of life. I. Title.
BJ1571 .C55 2015

Cover design by Jonathan Ramsay

asburyseminary.edu
800.2ASBURY
204 North Lexington Avenue
Wilmore, Kentucky 40390

First Fruits
THE ACADEMIC OPEN PRESS OF ASBURY SEMINARY

First Fruits Press
The Academic Open Press of Asbury Theological Seminary
204 N. Lexington Ave., Wilmore, KY 40390
859-858-2236
first.fruits@asburyseminary.edu
asbury.to/firstfruits

THE GREAT SECRET

HEALTH, BEAUTY, HAPPINESS, FRIEND-MAKING, COMMON SENSE, SUCCESS

BY

FRANCIS EDWARD CLARK, D.D.

President of the United Society of Christian Endeavor and of the World's Christian Endeavor Union

"The secret of the Lord is with them that fear him."

UNITED SOCIETY
OF CHRISTIAN ENDEAVOR
BOSTON   CHICAGO

𝔓𝔩𝔦𝔪𝔭𝔱𝔬𝔫 𝔓𝔯𝔢𝔰𝔰
Printers and Binders, Norwood, Mass.
U. S. A.

DEDICATED TO

𝔐. 𝔚. ℭ. and 𝔈. 𝔉. ℭ.

AND TO THE GREAT MULTITUDE
OF YOUNG MEN AND WOMEN
WHOM THEY REPRESENT,
WITH THE EARNEST HOPE AND PRAYER
THAT EACH ONE MAY LEARN
FOR HIMSELF

THE GREAT SECRET.

CONTENTS.

PREFACE.

THE object of this little book is to present some of the less obvious and less understood results of communion with God.

The fruits of the Spirit — love, joy, peace, long-suffering, kindness — are often, and rightly, dwelt upon as the supremely blessed outcome of the Spirit-filled life ; and yet there are other, and no less real, benefits which communion with God confers, which should not be left out of the account.

To be sure, if we seek God's presence for the sake of the health, friends, and

prosperity which it will bring, the bless-
ings will elude our selfish grasp, and
the precious secret will never be ours.
No sort of simony is tolerated by God.
But if we truly seek God for himself,
with himself he freely gives us all
things. If we seek first his kingdom
and his righteousness, all these things
shall be added.

I have made frequent use of this
phrase, "practising the presence of
God," so loved of Jeremy Taylor,
Brother Lawrence, and other devout
men, because the use of this somewhat
unusual synonym for communion with
God, and similar phrases, may lead some
of my readers to inquire more deeply
into its meaning, and to find out for
themselves its blessed significance.

These chapters have been written

during a long and otherwise tedious and unpleasant voyage of twenty-three days in tropical seas, on a Hindoo coolie ship, from India to South Africa, during which (for the voyage has been in some sense my Arabia) I trust I have learned something (more, at least, little as it is, than I ever knew before) of the blessed life I have tried to open to others.

Young people, especially, long with an intense longing to know the secret of true success in life; I have put into their hands the key. May God, who alone can do it, help them to unlock the wondrous secret.

Steamship "Congella,"
Indian Ocean, March, 1897.

THE
    GREAT
        SECRET

PART I.

                              THE
                                  SECRET
                                    OF
                                  HEALTH

THE GREAT SECRET.

PART I.

THE SECRET OF HEALTH.

"Art thou in health, my brother?"—2 Sam.
20 : 9.

HEALTH lies very near the foun-
dation of happiness and prosperity and beauty.   The chronic invalid is
seldom happy, and rarely successful or
comely.   Ill health is a fearful handicap
in life's race.   It weights its victim
with a fresh load at the beginning of
every new day, and, though a few rare
souls smile through the tears wrung

from them by the tortures of disease, and a few more have risen superior to physical suffering, and won a splendid success in life, yet these are but the exceptions, for life's coast-line is strewn with the wrecks of hope and happiness caused by physical disease.

No wonder, then, that a very considerable portion of man's invention and energy seems to be devoted to the twofold problem, how to get well, how to keep well.

Patent Remedies.

The advertising columns of our newspapers, our bill-boards, and fence-rails, give one answer to this question as they tell of nostrums, more or less valuable, for the different ills to which flesh is heir.

The sacred shrines, like those of Lourdes or St. Ann's or the Virgin of Guadalupe, give another answer and another illustration of the eagerness of men to leave their crutches and their diseases behind them, and to stand upon their feet, whole and sound. The votary of Christian science offers another panacea, and one which has this great merit, that it strenuously exalts mind over matter, the spiritual over the material; but it is mixed, if I may express a humble opinion, with not a few erroneous or partial views of truth.

The believer in faith-cure points out still another, but somewhat parallel, high road to health, which, though it seems sometimes, when trodden by the unbalanced and fanatical, to be a narrow and crooked thoroughfare, leading to the

lunatic asylum rather than to robust
and manly vigor, is yet worthy of sym-
pathetic study, in that its avowed end
is to lead those who follow it directly
to God.

I have no new nostrums to offer, no
new " cure " to advocate ; but I devoutly
believe that too little has always been
thought of the hygienic effect of communion with God.   I devoutly believe
that a multitude of physical diseases
might be arrested and a multitude more
cured by the constant, habitual " practice of the presence of God."

No Magic.

These cures would not be wrought
by magic or by miracle, but strictly in
accordance with the immutable laws of
nature, which are the laws of God.

This theory would not do away with the use of means or skilfully adminis- tered medicine; it would not set a broken limb without splints, or refuse to believe that vaccination prevents small-pox; but it would go directly as well as indirectly to Him who is the giver of health and every good and per- fect gift.

Take, for instance, the whole range of nervous diseases, whose name is legion. These diseases cause more suf- fering, and in these days, probably, are more widely prevalent than all others put together. What can be done for them? The wisest practitioners have been in despair. No known medicine can reach their root. The prescribed tonics do but brace and stimulate, and often leave the man in his last estate seven times worse than in his first.

Travel, recreation, change of place, do but keep the pain. Exercise and electricity, massage and movement cures, at the most only palliate; they do not remove the disease.

What, then, is to be done? Shall we give up in despair, and let nervous prostration claim a thousand times more victims than plague and cholera? Shall we give the New World over to be increasingly a prey to " Americanitis," as nervous collapse has been called?

The Rest Cure.

No; the wisest physicians who have made a lifelong study of the nerves and their ailments have united in the conclusion that there is one effective remedy, — the rest cure. If for weeks or months the patient can be induced to rest his body and his mind absolutely, as a little child rests in its mother's arms, he will in all probability recover. In God alone — I say it with all reverence — we find the real rest cure, for he alone is the source of rest. He alone gives rest to the nervously weary and heavy-laden. He is the rest as well as the refuge of his saints. In him alone the *soul* can rest, and thus he becomes "the health of our countenance."

To talk of the "rest cure" to the wealthy may be well enough, but to many a man it is but a mockery. How can he take the "rest cure" who has nothing in the bank, with wife and children dependent on him for daily bread? But upon God he can lay his heavy burdens, and in his everlasting arms he can rest, even though he must every morning arise and go to his grinding toil.

Even the millionaire can buy only physical rest, and that is the smallest part of the "cure." With a bank full of gold he cannot purchase freedom from care and the torments of anxiety and worry, which more than all other causes produce nervous prostration. Yea, the bank full of gold and the care it entails are the most prolific sources of the disease he is fighting. How can he find rest? Not in bed, not in a holiday, not in Europe. Like the poorest clerk in his own bank, he can find real rest and permanent relief only in God, in casting the bank and all its heavy cares on him.

What is true of the protean monster called nervous prostration is true of many another disease. The sick child puts its little burning hand into its mother's cool and steady palm, and its fever abates, and it drops off into a healing sleep. So the sick child of larger growth, when he has come into the same loving relation with his Father in heaven, when he practises constantly his presence, consciously, even if figuratively, places his hand in his Father's (he can express the spiritual act in no better way), and the fever abates. The consciousness of strength and confidence and repose come over him, and the telltale temperature thermometer would often mark the difference, and show that, attacked by the same fever, the trustful child of God had a far better chance of life than the anxious, choleric, impatient fellow patient, who trusted only in quinine and calomel.

Thus by removing anxiety fever is allayed and inflammation reduced, and the diseased lung or brain or the broken limb more quickly becomes sound and well.

It is a fact too well known to need further statement that infectious diseases most often attack those who fear them most. Two men may walk through the same hospital where cholera rages, and the man who is serene and confident in the presence of God and in the consciousness that he himself is in the way of duty is far more secure than the nervous, timid soul who fears that every moment he may contract disease.

The Secret Told.

But I have said enough, perhaps, to make my meaning clear. I am not speaking in a figurative, symbolic way about God as the source of health. I would be taken literally. The blood thermometer and the stethoscope, the microscope searching for microbes, and the doctor's practised ear listening to the pulsations of the heart would recognize the difference, other things being equal, between a man who practised the presence of God and a man who did not.

Annuity computations and life-insurance tables, could they but take this factor into account, would be affected thereby, and "His saving health" would be "known among all nations."

Why should this be thought a thing incredible? He came into the world that we might have life, and *that we might have it more abundantly ;* and physical life and health are dependent on spiritual life and health.

How can we practise in this school of medicine? By practising the pres- ence of God. And this involves the renunciation of known sin, though it be like the cutting off of the right hand or the plucking out of the right eye. It involves the complete surrender of one's self to God, the giving up of one's will to him, the " willingness to be made willing," if you can get no further at first. It involves the taking of time every day to commune with God, be- ing alone with him ; opening the whole being to him; taking suggestions and directions directly from him, and living up to every known duty.

Is all this a difficult task, a hard school of medicine in which to practise? O my brother, you will not find it so. You will soon find it your greatest joy to practise the presence of God who healeth all thy diseases.

THE
GREAT
SECRET

PART II.

THE
SECRET
OF
BEAUTY

PART II.

THE SECRET OF BEAUTY.

"Let the beauty of the Lord our God be upon us." — Ps. 90 : 17.

TO seek to have a beautiful face is no unworthy aspiration; the object of attaining beauty and the means of attaining it alone may make the quest ignoble.

It is a platitude that will bear repetition that comeliness is attractive, and to be attractive is to win people to your way of thinking and living.

Every one should set before himself a high ideal, and then seek to become a powerful magnet to attract all others to that ideal.

The young woman who neglects her natural charms and, from a false ascetic notion, becomes unkempt, repulsive, or unattractive in personal appearance, neglects a gift that is in her, and needs to ponder Paul's advice to Timothy.

The young man who becomes slovenly and slipshod, and neglectful of personal appearance, shows, so far forth, a certain demoralization of character. There is almost more hope of a " dude " than of him. A limp Bible in the hands is an excellent thing ; but it is robbed of something of its power when it goes with a limp collar, a greasy waistcoat, or a beard of four days' growth.

But I need not urge these views. There is no woman, and there are few

men, who in their secret hearts do not
desire comeliness of feature and form.
The question is how to attain this
grace.

A Beauty within the Reach of All.

It is very evident that some elements
of beauty, usually considered essential,
are not within the reach of all.   Not
every one can have the sparkling eye,
the rosy cheek, the pearly teeth, the
luxuriant hair of just the right shade,
over which novelists go into raptures.
If these properties make up the full
inventory of beauty, then it can be only
the coveted prize of the few, and not
the common possession of the many.
But it is just because these qualities
do not make real beauty, just because
beauty is a thing to be attained, some-

thing made and not born, that this chapter is written.

It is a very old and trite saying, but as true as are most trite sayings, that beauty is a matter of the soul and of character. The fact that needs to be made very plain is that the body comes in time to express the character, accurately, exactly, inevitably. The beautiful soul must in time come to look out through beautiful eyes. The beautiful character is sure to express itself, sooner or later, in a beautiful smile, in a charming expression, that makes the whole face lovely.

"Handsome is that handsome does," is a homely proverb that means a great deal more than is commonly supposed. Not only is it true that a beautiful act is itself beautiful; but, often repeated, it makes beautiful the character, and eventually the face, of the doer.

Ugly Is That Ugly Does.

The converse of this is sadly true. Ugly is that ugly does. Every stroll upon a crowded city street confirms it. Look into the faces of those you meet, and upon how many you will see avarice, duplicity, frivolity, lust, debauchery, imprinted as with a hot branding-iron! The soul has stamped its impress there, and the unconscious passer-by shows the world, as if he held up a printed page, that the soul within is marring and defacing its outward temple.

That we may see very plainly how the face expresses the soul, and becomes beautiful or ugly as the soul is beautiful or ugly, consider the faces of two girls whom it is not hard to picture. Very likely we have all actually known such girls.

One begins life with what people call a beautiful face. The features are regular, the eyes bright, the complexion fair and flawless, the hair abundant and glossy. Passing strangers stop to admire her, and say, "What a pretty little girl!"

The other girl, her playmate, attracts no attention; her features are not strikingly attractive; she is just an everyday little girl, of whom no one takes much notice. Her playmate wins all the praise, and if any one notices her, it is only to say, "She is a plain little thing." But the days go by, and every day leaves its mark upon each little face. A suspicion of pride and vanity begins to gleam out of the pretty girl's eyes; an unlovely pout is easily called to the corners of her lips; an expression of sarcastic selfishness takes up its abode in her dimpled cheeks. Men instinctively avoid her, warned, unconsciously, by some good genius within. As the years go by, these little lines, at first so faint, are graven more deeply; as age approaches, they are frightfully accentuated, and she becomes, in the eyes of every one, an unlovely old woman.

The Plain Girl Grows Comely.

The other one, the plain girl, somehow develops an attractive winsomeness. Eyes, mouth, and cheeks are the same as at first, yet not the same. A good fairy seems to have touched every feature while she slept, and to have irradiated it. It is, indeed, the good fairy of a sweet disposition and an unselfish soul. Gentleness looks out of her eyes, happiness and good nature curves her lips, and peace seems to brood over her whole sunny face. It is a face that wise young men wish to win for their own, for hers is a beauty that satisfies the soul as well as the eyes.

But this is just the beauty that can be cultivated, as the gardener cultivates and develops a rare flower. It is not dependent upon parentage and lineage. It is not a thing of complexion or sparkle or regularity; still less is it a matter of rouge and crimps and powder. It is a beauty that will wash and wear. Better than all, it is within the reach of all.

Some of us, when we look in the glass, are painfully impressed with the fact that the artist would never take us for his model. We are, moreover, shy and bashful and ill at ease, and add awkwardness of manner to awkwardness of feature; but there is a great Artist, the Creator of every living thing, who will transform and transfigure us if we will let him.

The Secret Told.

The Christlike spirit always looks out through beautiful eyes. Christ's smile always rests on beautiful lips. The secret of beauty, would you know it? It is the same as the secret of health. Practise the presence of God. Dwell much upon his character and his loveliness as revealed in Jesus Christ. Go by yourself every day to talk with God. Search your heart to see that pride and envy and anger and lust and covetousness, all of which leave their ugly creases upon the face, have no abiding-place in your soul. Seek to be like him in every half-unconscious act, in every passing thought, and little by little his beautiful image will be impressed upon your face as well as on your heart. As you come to see him more and more as he is, you come to be like him.

Again I must remind my readers that I am not writing figuratively and rhetorically, but what I believe are practical words of truth and soberness. *To practise the presence of God is to grow beautiful in face.* To commune with him is to become attractive and lovable and winsome.

Not for this beauty in itself, of course, should we practise his presence. To do this from the wrong motive would defeat our very purpose, and ugly selfishness, not the beauty of Christlikeness, would be reflected in our faces. But he who in love and lowliness looks into God's face at length is seen to have in his own face the love and gentleness and grace of God, and the peace which passeth understanding.

THE
  GREAT
    SECRET

PART III.

THE
  SECRET
    OF
      HAPPINESS

PART III.

THE SECRET OF HAPPINESS.

"In thy presence is fulness of joy."—Ps.
16: 11.

HAPPINESS, as usually sought, is the most elusive of emotions. When we think we have it most securely caged, we find that it has escaped us and flown to another bush. Its secret, more eagerly desired than any other, plays constant hide-and-seek with the ardent wooer, and remains a secret.

To many persons it seems that there are two kinds of happiness, the happiness of the without, and the happiness of the within, and, the happiness of the without being to them the most real and obvious, they seek for it with feverish eagerness. They pursue it to the mountains and the seashore. They cross the ocean to find it in Europe. They seek it in the theatre and the dance-hall. If of a domestic turn of mind, they look for it by the hearth-rug and the fireside, and seek to establish a home and build up an estate. If of literary inclination, they seek this will-o'-the-wisp in books and communion with the spirits of the past. The mere man of business hopes to find it in his bank and counting-room, and cannot imagine it apart from ledgers and day-books.

But all these methods of seeking happiness, from the coarse, animal pleasure of the libertine, to the refined, æsthetic pleasure of the artist, have this fatal defect in common, that they look for it *without* the man, in *things*, things that may or may not be right in themselves, but that have as little happiness inhering in them as the refuse heap of a city " dump."

As I write these words, I am pursued by the fear that many of my readers will impatiently skip this letter, saying : " O, yes, we have heard this before. It is the old story that the minister and the moralist are always telling." But, if it is an old story, it is a true story, and none the worse — nay, all the better — for its age, for this shows the consensus of many minds in many ages.

Within, Not Without.

But whether old or new, fresh or stale, received as a glad revelation or

scorned as an ancient platitude, it remains certain that the secret spring of
happiness must be sought *within*. He
will never, never know the secret who
seeks it elsewhere.

This truth can be easily illustrated.
A man travels far to see some wonder
of nature of which he has long dreamed,
and to behold which, he imagines, will
fill him with rapturous joy. Perhaps it
is the falls of Niagara. But, when he
reaches Niagara, a telegram is given
him, saying that some business venture
has gone wrong and half his property is
swept away. Would the man of the
world enjoy the magnificent glories of
the cataract with that telegram in his
hand?

Niagara would be just as majestic, as
awe-inspiring, as ever, but it would have

few beauties for that man, for he could not look at it with an unruffled heart. There would be a cloud, denser than the mist that rises from the falls, between him and the glories of the mighty cataract.

Here is another man, who has set his heart upon being a millionaire. During weary years of money-grubbing and muck-raking, he has said to himself, "When I am worth a million, I shall be supremely happy." The day his ambition is realized, however, he learns from the doctor that he has an incurable disease, which within a twelvemonth will surely carry him to the grave. Do you believe he is a happy man? He has all that he set his heart upon. The million dollars is his, indubitably, well invested and secure; but, with the terrible news of the inevitable end so near, he cannot smile at his money-bags, and the healthy boy whistling along the village street, without a nickel in his pocket, is happier far than the millionaire.

Why is this ?   Because happiness lies not in beautiful Niagara, but in the soul behind the eye that looks at Niagara. Because happiness is found not in a million dollars' worth of safe securities, or in all that the million dollars will buy, but in the soul of the man that owns the securities.

What Makes Niagara Beautiful.

On the other hand, it requires no stretch of the imagination to conceive of a devout and heavenly-minded Christian, serene and happy, under exactly similar circumstances.

His property gone? "The Lord gave, and the Lord hath taken away; blessed be the name of the Lord," he says. His days numbered? He is not dismayed, for he can shout triumphantly: "For we know that if our earthly house of this tabernacle be dissolved, we have a building from God, a house not made with hands, eternal, in the heavens. . . . Therefore we are always confident."

"But," says the objector, "men do not always lose their property when they gaze at Niagara, or always lose their health when they make a million dollars." Undoubtedly; but the truth I would make plain, a truth we are all slow to learn, but without which we can never know the secret, is that happiness lies in the man himself, and not in the

thing outside the man.   If he is happy
when he looks, Niagara gives him pleasure, but not otherwise.   If he is happy
when he contemplates his stocks and
bonds, they contribute to his joy, but
his happiness may be quite apart from
them.

There is, then, but one place to look
for happiness, and that is within the
soul itself.   The spring must be found
there, or else it cannot well up to flood
the life.

An Amazon of Happiness.

But, thank God, every son of man
can have it implanted within him.
There is none so poor, so obscure, so
dull, so cross-grained by nature, so un-
fortunate, so sickly, so friendless, so
weighted by circumstances, that he

cannot have, flowing through his life, the streams which " make glad." As there are vast underground rivers in many parts of the world, broader and deeper and of more majestic sweep than any Mississippi or Amazon, streams which men may often tap and bring to the surface in ever-flowing artesian wells, so there is an undercurrent of happiness in this universe, and if we connect our lives with it, our joy is perennial ; there shall be within us then a well of water, springing up not only unto everlasting life, but to everlasting happiness.

This undercurrent of happiness, or, rather, — let us give it its nobler name, —of blessedness, is *God.* How shall you obtain it ? Connect yourself with God. Practise the presence of God. This is the secret, the only secret, of happiness. Enter into the secret of his pavilion. Go by yourself every morning for this infilling of the indwelling God. Open wide your heart's doors to him. Leave no dark, cobweb-lined room in your soul, which you shut away from him. Find out what John has to tell you about the Holy Spirit, about his abiding, ever-indwelling, informing, enlightening, comforting presence. Do not only know *about* it, but know it; know *him*, as a matter, not of books and second-hand information, but of experience. Then you have learned the secret of happiness.

Again, lest my readers think I am using common words in an occult, mystical sense, let me say that I am talking about ordinary, every-day happiness, the very thing that we are all seeking, the element in life which makes it worth living. There are not two kinds of happiness. There is only one. There are many kinds of distraction, many ways of filling up the time; only one way of filling the heart.

As the setting sun lights up the heavens and makes the darkest clouds radiant with supernal glory, so the happy heart lights up everything upon which the eyes rest. Niagara becomes more glorious, the home hearthstone more lovely, the Alps more majestic, travel more enchanting, home-staying more charming, success more sweet, sorrow more salutary, and our very tears become prisms through which we behold irradiated the brighter purposes of God.

I began by saying that happiness of a certain sort is the most elusive of emotions ; let me close by saying that the happiness which comes from practising the presence of God is the most steady and abiding of realities. It can always be had. It is always at hand. It never eludes the honest seeker. It never deserts him in the hour of crisis, for it is wherever and whenever God is, and God is always and everywhere. And, O blessed thought! it may be yours and mine to-day and forever.

THE
  GREAT
    SECRET

PART IV.

THE
  SECRET
    OF
FRIEND-MAKING

PART IV.

THE SECRET OF FRIEND-MAKING.

"I have called you friends." — JOHN 15: 15.

THERE is within most hearts an intense longing for friendship. If friendship is not the " master passion," it is certainly one of the ruling passions of the soul. Even those who usually appear to others most indifferent or most forbidding are often simply trying to conceal under a cold exterior their shyness or their real longing for the love of others. Under such human masks, which bring one the credit — or the discredit — of being haughty and self-contained, often seethes a very vol-

cano of pent-up longing for human sym-
pathy and affection.

A genuine friendship philter, which
should compel the regard of others,
would be the most popular drug in the
market.

Then why is this treasure, which is
so earnestly desired by all mankind, and
is within the reach of all, not more often
found ?

The answer is obvious. It is not
sought in the right place or in the right
way. You may seek for gold a hun-
dred years in New Hampshire's granite
hills or in the deep loam of Iowa's prai-
ries, but you will not find it in paying
quantities, because it is not there. But,
if you go to Colorado's hills or to the
Rand of the Transvaal, to the quartz-
mines of Ballarat or the alluvial fields

of the Klondike, you will find the precious yellow metal you seek.

Seeking Gold.

You may search even there with a
garden rake and a wood-chopper's axe,
and you will not be likely to find it.
You must take pick and crowbar and
dynamite cartridge and stamping-mill
before your search will be amply re-
warded.

So we seek the secret of friendship
in the wrong place and in the wrong
way. We seek it in ourselves or in
others, where it is not to be found.

"But where," you say, "is it to be
found, if not in one or both of the two
people who alone are concerned?"

Here is just our fallacy. More than
two are concerned. God is concerned,

and the source and secret of friendship we must find in him. Many have had some such experience as this: They have ardently longed for some human friendship, which seemed to them almost indispensable to life. But they could not find their way into the longed-for affectionate regard. There was always some obstacle which prevented the progress of their craft into the secure, unruffled harbor of perfect confidence and esteem. Some awkwardness of manner, some lack of grace or refinement, some stupidity or blunder, or lack of conversational power, kept them outside the bar they longed to cross.

The Invisible Friendship.

Let such a one make no further frantic, futile attempts to cross the bar, but

seek in God himself the secret of friendship, for the sake, not of the earthly
friendship, but of the divine. Seeking
the divine friendship, he will become
like the divine One, and he will find
in Jesus Christ the image of the invisible friendship as well as of the
invisible power and glory. He will
become thoughtless of self as he learns
that even Christ pleased not himself.
He will become careful of others' rights
and others' feelings. He will learn
something of the blessedness of the
meek, of the peacemaker, of the pure
in heart; and in his life will be obeyed
that injunction which sounds like a soft,
sweet strain of music whenever we hear
it : "Be ye kind one to another, tender-
hearted, forgiving one another, even as
God for Christ's sake hath forgiven
you."

Can any one conceive of such a man's being friendless? It is impossible. Any friendship in this wide world that is worth having would be at the disposal of a really Christlike man. He would not have to seek for it. It would be his by a law as irresistible as that which draws the soft iron to the magnet, the bee to the honey-filled flower, the planet to the sun around which it revolves. Only the hardened and wilfully vicious could resist the attraction of such a man.

It has been said with truth, "The world does not yet know what God can accomplish through a fully consecrated man." It is equally true that the world does not yet know the supreme attractiveness and love-compelling power of a thoroughly Christlike, thoroughly unselfish, life.

"The Soft Face."

We have, to be sure, many measur-
able approaches to this perfection. Our
lives have all been blessed and sweetened by such characters. That popular
writer, J. M. Barrie, in his exquisite
biography of his mother, Margaret Ogil-
vie, heads one chapter, "How my mother
got her soft face." As the book goes
on, he often hints at its true source.
She found her "soft face" on her
knees, where the children often sur-
prised her. Many another mother, the
mother whom some of us have known,
has found her soft and shining face in
the same lowly place.

The secret of friendship is the secret
of an unselfish life; not merely the unselfishness that is continually *doing* for
others, cooking and sewing and crochet-

ing, and preparing delicacies, but the deeper unselfishness that forgets self, that gets us out of self and gets self out of us.

The reason why we are not popular with others in the best sense of the word is that we are too self-conscious. We never have "a mind at leisure from itself." We are always thinking what will make us great or rich or happy. We are ever considering how we shall appear before others. We are ever thinking of our likes or dislikes, of our honor or dignity, of our rights or wrongs. No wonder we find the art of friend-making so difficult an art.

The best manual for the friend-maker is found in the thirteenth chapter of First Corinthians, where he learns that love (and love is the chief ingredient of friendship) is long-suffering and kind, not envious or rash or puffed up, not unseemly in behavior ; that she "*seeketh not her own,*" "*is not easily provoked,*" and "*thinketh no evil.*"

But these rare qualifications, which must be possessed in greater or less degree to make friendship possible, are found in their full perfection in God alone.

Let us, then, go back to the fountain-head. Would you be a friend and have friends ? Then practise the presence of God. Seek in him the elements of true friendship. Spend much time with him. Begin the day and close it alone with him. Seek in the likeness and life of Christ the elements which made him the friend of sinners, and you, too, will have learned the art of friend-making.

The highest title ever applied to man has not been won by any duke or earl or king or emperor, but was won by an old Eastern sheik named Abraham. He was called "The Friend of God." He who practises the presence of God becomes the friend of God, and the friend of God has learned the secret of friendship.

THE
GREAT
SECRET

PART V.

THE
SECRET
OF
COMMON SENSE

PART V.

THE SECRET OF COMMON SENSE.

"The manifold wisdom of God."— EPH. 3 : 10.

IT has been said that common sense is the most uncommon sense. And so it seems when we search history or the ways of common people in common life. They have everything else that is common except common sense.

The greatest geniuses have often lacked this saving grain of salt in their character. Napoleon, for instance, intoxicated by continued success, and by his own selfish, intolerable ambition, committed at last, in his march to Moscow, the fatal mistake from which a man of less genius but more common sense would have been saved, and his star from that moment began to wane. Washington in military genius was a dwarf compared with Napoleon, but he was a man of saving common sense, and he won a more imperishable re-nown. Lincoln, gaunt, grave, homely, towering Lincoln, the great future hero of the nineteenth century, united with the rarest genius of heart and soul more uncommon common sense than any man of his generation ; and for this he will be remembered and loved when other presidents and rulers are but mere names on the pages of dusty history.

What Is Common Sense?

But common sense is not a quality that only warriors and statesmen need.

We must all have it in order to do our
life-work well. The schoolboy needs it
in the classroom, the housewife in the
kitchen, the minister needs it in study
and pulpit, the merchant behind the
counter, the farmer in the field, the
artisan in the shop, the doctor on his
rounds. What is it? It is a rare com-
bination of many ingredients. It is tact.
It is foresight. It is quickness to divine
the right. It is an intuitive adaptation
of means to ends. It is all this and
more. It makes all the difference between success and failure, between a
fatal defeat and a glorious victory.

Especially does a young Christian,
for his own peace of mind and for his
Master's glory, need this gift of common
sense to balance and steady him. If he
has it not, the very intensity of his con-

viction is apt to lead him into extravagance and fanaticism.   He becomes
convinced, perhaps, of the truth of
some controverted and non - essential
doctrine and custom ; and these views,
held not in due proportion and subordi-
nation to more important truths, fill the
whole segment of his horizon.   He can
think, speak, write, of nothing else.   He
offends his neighbor's reverence for the
first day of the week, refuses to call a
physician for his dying child, prepares
his ascension robes and gives away his
property because of a private interpre-
tation of some obscure chapter in Dan-
iel.   Scandal is brought upon the cause
he loves and the name of the Lord he
adores, for lack of the saving element
of common sense among his Christian
graces.

Lack of Balance.

Or this lack may be shown in other ways. Inflated schemes of Christian work may seem reasonable. Bloated plans for revolutionizing society and bringing about the millennium are eagerly pursued, and never abandoned, even when their absurdity is exposed. Lack of Christian boldness and a faith that dares no great things for God is deplorable; but equally deplorable is the lack of balance and the foolish intrepidity which runs before it is sent, and makes Christianity a laughing-stock before a gainsaying world.

There are some good men, whom we all know, who seem to possess every other virtue but this. They are eloquent, witty, wise, but they are not well balanced. They possess a su-

preme faculty for botching and blunder-
ing.   They are boastful or extravagant
in statement.   They joke at a funeral,
or by ill-timed facetiousness seek to
dissipate a friend's grief.   They do the
right thing at the wrong time.   Their
mortified friends sum up their character
by saying, "They have everything but
common sense."

This seems more like a radical, fun-
damental defect of character than almost
any other.   But even this is not incurable.   Common sense, too, is not only
born, but made.   Study will not make
it ; friends cannot do much ; experience
often seems to teach but little ; but
there is a course of spiritual schooling
which has often accomplished won-
ders for those who lack "this grace
also."

God Holds the Key.

It is the same old, but wondrously
new, secret. God himself holds the
key. He hath said, " If any of you
lack wisdom, let him ask of God, that
giveth to all men liberally, and upbraid-
eth not." Then let us go to him if we
feel our need, and claim the fulfilment
of this promise. Practise the presence
of God. Spend much time alone with
him. Lay before him your mistakes,
your strange lack of success, the elusive
hopes almost realized, but always dashed
by some fatal blunder, a blunder which
you cannot understand, but which your
friends call a lack of common sense.
Lay before him every new plan, every
doubtful scheme, every address or letter,
every ardent wish for service.

And the result ? The boundaries of

your thinking will be rectified.   You will no longer be spiritually blear-eyed or squint-eyed.   You will see things in their true proportions and relations. You will unconsciously come to measure by God's rule and weigh by his balances. You will know the trivial from the important, the temporary from the transient, the passing from the eternal. You will "see clear and think straight." Thus extravagance will be pruned, a trifling theory will not be exalted into an eternal truth ; the word will come to fit the thought ; the means adopted will be suited to the end to be gained.   You will no longer kill gnats with trip-hammers, or strive to empty the sea with a tin cup.   In short, you will learn to do your work modestly, quietly, effectively, happily, wisely, well ; and what is this but the exercise of uncommon common sense ?

All this is the blessed experience, as the record of many a wise and successful Christian worker has proved, of the man who practises much the presence of God.

THE
  GREAT
    SECRET

PART VI.

THE
  SECRET
   OF
  SUCCESS

PART VI.

THE SECRET OF SUCCESS.

"Then thou shalt have good success." — JOSH.
1 : 8.

THE secret of success is, in the opinion of most men, the secret of secrets. To this they regard everything else as tributary; health and friends and common sense are good only as they win something they call success in life. All that a man hath will he give for success; even life itself is held cheap by many, so long as life's dear, coveted prize is won.

And those who reason thus are not far wrong. They are wrong, if at all, only in their conception of what true success is.

What, then, is the definition of this all-comprehensive word of magic, "success," to achieve which conquerors have often waded in blood, and many an ungifted man has worn out his body and bartered his soul?

It may be defined as the attaining of one's cherished aims and life-purposes. Then, whether success is noble or ignoble, worthy or paltry, depends upon the question whether these life-purposes are worthy or paltry.

"How do you manage to get such a weally wemarkable knot in your tie, Chollie, old fellow?" a gilded youth, according to one of our comic papers, asks another; and "Chollie" replies, "Well, I fling me whole soul into it, doncher see?"

Undoubtedly success in cravat-tying can be thus achieved, but the question is apt to arise, "Is it worth while, after all?"

Is It Worth While?

The young man who spent all his spare time for five years in teaching a poodle dog to stand on its hind legs and balance a penny on its nose succeeded, but was the success worth achieving? The fabled professor who spent his whole life upon the dative case of the Greek article doubtless became a learned man concerning the Greek dative, but was his success worth achieving? The housewife who scrubs and scours and scrapes and polishes her dishes and her brassware and her floors, instead of polishing her own wits and those of her children, undoubtedly achieves success as a notable housewife, and comes to have an immaculate and spotless house; but if hers is only a house, and not a true *home*, is her success worth achieving? The man who becomes a slave to his business, who grows gray and wrinkled in soul as well as body, who dulls his finer sensibilities, and becomes at last a mere money-making machine, usually succeeds in piling up a large bank account, but is his success worth achieving?

So we might go on through a long, long list of life-purposes, on whose achievement men have set their hearts and risked their souls; and again and again the questions would recur: "Is it worth while?" "Is such success worth achieving?" And in every case the mournful answer would come back: "No, no, no. This success, when won, isn't worth the winning." Those who had most completely gained such a life's purpose would be the first to give this answer.

The One True Success.

Thus, as we went on, ever asking this question, and ever receiving the same answer, we should be driven by an inexorable process of elimination to this conclusion: There is only one that can fill full the insatiable soul of man, and that is God. There is but one life-purpose whose achievement is real success, and that is the pursuit of the knowledge of God. There is but one complete satisfaction, and that is the satisfaction of awaking in his likeness.

It follows, then, that no other success is worth the achieving which is not knowledge of God and likeness to God.

But this success, O discouraged brother man, this success of successes, is within *your* grasp. You may have missed the secret of wealth or power or fame; but this, which is worth them all, ten million times over, is yours if you will have it. It is the same open secret about which we have talked in the other chapters, and the method of attaining it is the same. Seek Him who will ever be found of those who seek him. Practise the presence of God. Seek this supreme success alone, in your chamber, the door closed even on your dearest earthly friend, and the door of your heart closed to all but God. You will take your Bible with you. It will open almost of itself to certain passages in John's Gospel and Paul's and John's epistles. It will be no mere printed book. It will be your Father's letter, your Father's love-letter, if we may redeem the word from trivial associations. But you will not always even read his letter; you will talk with him as a man talketh with a friend. You will ask him questions and hear his answer. You will open to him the soul which he alone can fill; and, as more and more it becomes the supreme aim of your life to be God-filled, more and more will your life - purpose be gratified, and the supremest success will be yours.

Even the Lower Success.

Even lower and partial successes, I believe, are more likely to come to the

man who communes with God.   This is
inevitable, if, as I have claimed in pre-
vious chapters, communion with God
brings health and comeliness and friends
and happiness and common sense; for
it might be said in a lower, but very
real, sense that health and comeliness
and happiness and friends are the elements that constitute success.   Other
things being equal, given the same
brain-power, foresight, prudence, per-
severance, I believe the man who practises the presence of God is far more
likely to achieve, in the long run, mere
worldly success, to become the rich
man, the honored man, the powerful
man; for communion with God clarifies
the mind, steadies the nerves, dispels
the fog of prejudice, calms the fever
of envy and ill will, which often make

even the lowest form of success unat-
tainable.

But this success, if gained, is only
incidental and tributary; it only enables
us to serve God with larger power and
influence. It is not in itself the highest
success or necessary to the highest success. Let us bring our minds back to
the one plain, indisputable fact which
the history of every human soul reit-
erates. There is but one being large
enough to fill the soul of the puniest
man. It is God.

There is but one supreme aim, the
attainment of which means success. It
is God.

There is but one life-purpose worth
achieving. It is God.

A synonym which I think perhaps
John would use for success is his fa-

vorite word, "*life.*" And surely they mean much the same. Abundant life is abundant success. Eternal life is eternal success, for it is eternal likeness to God. Listen to our Lord's own definition of life. "This is life eternal, that they might know thee the only true God, and Jesus Christ, whom thou hast sent."

O God, give unto us all this life, by giving unto us thyself; for thou didst come to earth that we might have life, and that we might have it more abundantly.

THE
  GREAT
    SECRET

PART VII

WHAT IS IT
_{TO}
PRACTISE THE
PRESENCE OF GOD?

PART VII.

WHAT IS IT TO PRACTISE THE PRESENCE OF GOD?

PERHAPS, since I have used the phrase so persistently, I ought to explain more fully what I mean by "practising the presence of God," and how his presence may be practised.

I have used the phrase because, as I first saw it in the works of Jeremy Taylor and Brother Lawrence, it opened to my vision a whole new continent of truth, and I have hoped it might flash upon other minds the same blessed prospect, just as a stroke of lightning reveals a wide, but hitherto hidden, scene. In every article of this series I have tried to indicate briefly what practising the presence of God is.

But let me be more explicit. It involves going away by one's self. It involves a daily quiet hour with God. It involves a putting away of all known sin. It involves a searching of the heart for the rebellious life-guard who would keep some of the apartments of the soul closed to the entrance of the King.

Alas, in the case of most of us it needs but little searching; for we know the besetting sin, the favorite idol, which keeps God out, and we lack the will to cast it out of our hearts. But this is indispensable. We cannot practise the presence of God while *cherished* sin is there.

We must also give everything into God's care and keeping, and accept his will for our will. If we cannot at first honestly and fully do this, as has been wisely and well said, we can be " willing to be made willing" to give up everything for God.

Then, when thus the heart is made ready by the Holy Spirit, who always works with us in this preparation, let us yet longer sit still before God alone. Our Bible is open, perhaps to the familar passage which reveals the wondrous truth that man dwells in God and God in man, as John records it.

Seek to realize this stupendous fact, for all Scripture is a lie if this is not a fact.

Say to yourself over and over again : " GOD IS HERE. GOD IS HERE. GOD

IS WITHIN ME. *I am his child.* GOD
IS MY FATHER."

One of these thoughts is soul-food
enough for one day. Live on it
throughout that day, whenever in the
midst of daily duties an unoccupied
moment enables you to resort to it.

The next morning, for a half-hour's
meditation, take another of these biblical
truths. It may aid the sluggish spirit
at first to write out these short but
wondrous sentences in large capitals.

GOD IS HERE.

I AM GOD'S CHILD.

I AM IN MY FATHER'S PRES-
ENCE.

But we shall not always need the
written or printed sentence, for it will
soon be engraved on our souls and
become part of our lives.

Little by little we shall go on to appreciate by such communion and meditation the deep truths of God's incarnation in Jesus Christ, of the Holy Spirit's indwelling, enlightening, witnessing, comforting power. But it will all be God, God within and God without, God here, God everywhere, God in his word, in his world, in history, in us. We have come to realize, to *practise* (there is no other word so good) the presence of God. We look forward to the hour of this practice with supreme delight. It is refreshment, food, drink, clothing, health, to our soul.

Gradually the influence of the hour goes with us through the day; every sorrow is sweetened, every joy doubled, every care is lightened, by his presence. Service becomes sweet, difficult tasks easy. Every hour has its song; life becomes worth living.

Let me close by quoting the experience of Brother Lawrence, the poor monk, who knew as few men have done what it is to practise the presence of God.

Being questioned by one of his own society by what means he had attained such an habitual sense of God, he told him "that in the beginning he spent the hours appointed for private prayer in thinking of God, so as to convince his mind of, and to impress deeply upon his heart, the divine existence; . . . that by this short and sure method he exercised himself in the knowledge and love of God, resolving to use his utmost endeavor to live in a continual sense of his presence, and, if possible, never to forget him more."

" His very countenance," said his companion, was edifying, such a sweet and calm devotion appearing in it as could not but affect the beholders. And it was observed that in the greatest hurry of business in the kitchen (for he was a cook to the society), he still preserved his recollection and heavenly-mindedness. He was never hasty or loitering, but did each thing in its season, with an even, uninterrupted composure and tranquillity of spirit. "The time of business," said he, "does not with me differ from the time of prayer, and in the noise and clatter of my kitchen, while several persons are at the same time calling for different things, I possess God in as great tranquillity as if I were upon my knees at the blessed sacrament."

Here is a life, O Christian Endeavorers, that is not beyond our reach. We, too, can dwell in this atmosphere. We, too, can be hid in His pavilion. We, too, can practise the presence of God.

A Daily Message for Christian Endeavorers.

By Mrs. FRANCIS E. CLARK. With introduction by Dr. Clark. Beautifully illustrated. 384 pages. Price, only $1.00.

This is a book for the Quiet Hour, the Prayer Meeting, and the Birthday. It is three books in one. There is a page for every day in the year filled with the choicest thoughts of the best writers, that will enrich and deepen the spiritual life of every reader. The collection is the result of years of careful reading, and most of the selections will be found peculiarly appropriate for use in prayer meetings. The index of subjects will enable one to find choice quotations on almost any topic. A new feature in books of this kind is the place for birthday entries, space being given under every day in the year. The choicest gift-book of the year.

The Morning Watch.

A book for the Quiet Hour. By BELLE M. BRAIN. Cloth. About 400 pages. Price, $1.00.

Here are 366 diamonds of the rarest color and brilliancy, gems from the heart and brain and hand of the saints of God of all ages. With this book in your possession, you can live for a month and hold daily conversation with Andrew Murray, F. B. Meyer, A. J. Gordon, Francis E. Clark, D. L. Moody, J. R. Miller, and others. They will speak to you from the hours of their richest and deepest experience. If you want to draw near to God, you can have no better help than the daily message from his word and from his servant that this book will bring you.

PUBLISHING DEPARTMENT,
United Society of Christian Endeavor.

Tremont Temple,
Boston, Mass.

155 La Salle Street,
Chicago, Ill.

Elijah Tone, Citizen.

By AMOS R. WELLS. Cloth, illustrated, $1.00.
Paper covers, 25 cents.

This stirring and attractive story by Professor Wells will make a most acceptable gift for that wide-awake boy of yours; and if it interests the boys, you may be sure it will interest the girls. The theme is the nineteenth-century, up-to-date one of Christian citizenship, the characters are finely drawn, the situations are sufficiently thrilling, and the style so vigorous that it claims and holds the attention of the reader from the first page to the last. It ought to be in every Sunday school library.

Next Steps.

An advanced text-book in Christian Endeavor.
By Rev. W. F. McCAULEY. Cloth. 50 cents.

Here is a book for every Christian Endeavor worker. It is by the author of "How" and "Why," which have had so large a sale. It is a storehouse of suggestion. It deals not with theories, but with practical, workable methods. As a statement of Christian Endeavor principles and methods, it is unexcelled. If you want to help some earnest workers, make them a present of this book.

Sunday-School Success.

By AMOS R. WELLS. Cloth. Price, $1.25.

Professor Wells is an authority on Sunday-school work, and presents his ideas in so masterful a way that he grips the attention at once. Here is the freshest, most suggestive, and inspiring book for Sunday-school workers we have ever read. It ought to be in the hands of every superintendent and teacher. A splendid Christmas present for such workers.

PUBLISHING DEPARTMENT,

United Society of Christian Endeavor.

Tremont Temple,   155 La Salle Street,
Boston, Mass.   Chicago, Ill.

www.ingramcontent.com/pod-product-compliance
Lightning Source LLC
Chambersburg PA
CBHW020508030426
42337CB00011B/285